MW00884444

TO: KING
FROM:

SAMOSAS ARE SO YUMMY

by: asma sara ali

Copyright 2018 – Samosas Are So Yummy By: Asma Sara Ali
ISBN 9781985585560

All rights reserved. No part of this book may be reproduced, transmitted, or stored in an information retrieval system in any form or by any means, graphic. electronic, mechanical, including photocopying, taping, and recording, without prior written permission from the publisher.

For my nieces,

Maha and Ayesha

Samosas are so yummy.

I eat them all the time.

Aloo, keema or veggies.

No *chutney*? That's a crime!

Samosas are so yummy.

Mom always makes a lot.

For Eid, Ramadan and birthdays,

they sure do hit the spot!

Samosas are so yummy.

Triangular and fried.

They're crunchy when you bite them, filled with spicy flavors inside.

Samosas are so yummy.

Eat one and you'll agree.

I promise you'll find them delicious, let me share the recipe!

First you take some flour and water, then start to form a dough.

Make a filling with potatoes and spices, cook it together and it's ready to go!

Shape the dough into a triangle, add your mixture inside and fry!

Voila! You've got a samosa! You can make it if you try.

Some eat it with a *chaat*.

Some snack on it without.

One, two or three samosas, I can eat more no doubt.

Three is what I ate, when dad and I watched a game.

Then our team lost, so we had some more.

Eating samosas helps deal with the pain.

Samosas are so yummy.

I can't wait for you to have your first bite.

A plate full of samosas in front of you,

it will really be love at first sight!

But don't just look!

Have a taste and be sure to fill up your tummy.

After you do, you'll love to eat samosas because samosas are so yummy!

91880388R00018

Made in the USA
Columbia, SC
27 March 2018